Every Other Year is Odd

poems by

Karen Wingett

Finishing Line Press
Georgetown, Kentucky

Every Other Year is Odd

ACKNOWLEDGMENTS

Thank you to my sister Janet for sharing her love of literature with me and inspiring me every day she was alive; to my husband for his love and support; to my writing group for helping me shape these poems; and to my son, daughter-in-law and three granddaughters for encouraging me to tell my stories.

Publisher: Leah Maines
Editor: Christen Kincaid
Cover Art: Karen Wingett
Author Photo: Wes Wingett
Cover Design: Elizabeth Maines McCleavy

Printed in the USA on acid-free paper.
Order online: www.finishinglinepress.com
            also available on amazon.com

Author inquiries and mail orders:
Finishing Line Press
P. O. Box 1626
Georgetown, Kentucky 40324
U. S. A.

Table of Contents

Every Other Year is Odd

on my 33rd odd birthday i see
andy warhols exhibit in living
color in omaha strange and brilliant
on a cloudy day and write this poem
not using capitals or punctuation
not even leaving spaces so you know
where to take a breath I eat tiny white
cupcakes and cereal with milk for supper
while wes is smudged in india and eating
curry and getting love i get love too
from him and friends on facebook
a hundred well wishes and pals
who say im not invisible and a call
from my brotherinlaw who says happy
birthday and tells me about my sister
and her dementia because I ask
and want to know so I can understand
that i must appreciate life and show gratitude
for even the uneven year ahead.

Scalpel, Please

All will be black, I think, a week after
surgery (referring to the collage
I am creating) and white, gray, the pale
gold of ale—an artish job taking hours
and days to locate just-right photographs,
headlines, fonts, phrases from *The New Yorker*
and fairy tale volumes illustrated
grimly on crackling paper: wee pieces
capturing loss bleak and unexpected.
Lines will be stitched into pentameter
in the companion poem, cut bare, words
and syllables, entire stanzas snipped
out quietly with sterilized scissors
like body parts no longer fresh or useful
to what remains of the human poem.

Tonsillectomy

Sacred Heart's pediatric floor, serious,
clown-free, color-deprived in 1955
welcomes me to a bleachy bed. Suitcase
stored, new pajamas donned, I lie still
as my Ginny doll (dressed in her nurse's uniform)
faces me from her perch on the window sill.

In caps stiffly folded like linen napkins
at Bishop's Cafeteria, RNs turn off lights
leaving me alone to dream of white walls.

In the morning Dr. Abts says the Lord's Prayer
with me as he covers my nose with an ether cup
sending me into a den of green sleep.

I wake to nausea I never knew, vomiting
into a stainless kidney-shaped bowl
a small blood clot that looks like a cherry
Smith Brothers cough drop. I eat Jello,
hurt, have malts, cry, read my new
Jack and Jill magazine, wait for my parents.

I go home swallowing warily, newly acquainted
with lonely worlds where pain can stop or begin
in the prayer of a doctor.

Chance of a Lifetime

Maybe I was conceived in early March
on my father's 25th birthday after a night
of celebrations that hadn't ended yet,
only two years from the war where my dad
dreamed of home as he flew over Paris.

Maybe my parents had a quickie before
going to see *It Happened One Night*
at the Moon Theater on Walnut
or after listening to the radio broadcast
of the Nuremberg trials on the 10 o'clock news.

If I had been conceived on Christmas Eve
after opening presents, when my sister
stayed with her grandparents, I would have been
a Scorpio and started school when I was four.
I might be a boy named Karl or twin girls.

A phone call could have been *coitus interruptus:*
a hail storm, too many martinis. A headache or condom
could have reined me in. Then my granddaughters
would be someone's else's dream. Wes would have
a different bride. I would have no friends on Facebook,

and even Google couldn't locate me.

Troopers

Buckled into the backseat, the girls sip
from Capri Sun tutti frutti punch pouches
when flashing red and white lights startle
the bejesus out of them and me, Grandma,
with whom they were not expecting to have
their first encounter with The Law.

I have sped, it seems. Seventy-two
in a fifty-five. I answer questions.
Yes, I still live in Nebraska. I'm taking
my granddaughters across the Illinois
state line to shop (for Lucy's first middle
school dance, I want to say, but stifle myself.)

I peek in the mirror at the stunned girls.
Their bickering has stopped. Never have they been
so quiet. Never have I seen such wide-eyed
innocent looks. Shock. Nice Indy officer gives me
a warning (because of the sweet scene, I think.)
I drive relieved on, but They.Want.To.Know.

Has this happened before? What would the fine
have been? Why did he ask so many questions?
Why did I call Daddy? What did he say?
They.Want.To.Say. that they were really scared;
they will *never* forget it. For slow mile
after slow mile, they talk quietly
in a thrilled conspiracy about our
close encounter on Highway 40.

Let it Be

My great Irish aunts want me to go to heaven,
and from beyond the grave they comfort me
with the words of the Rosary unexpectedly
on the radio, *pray for us sinners now and at
the hour of our death.* Their beads are in my home;
the membership in the Purgatory Society
they bought for me, their prayer books,
Catholic Daughters membership cards,
pictures of popes. They send her here.

Though I am not Catholic, Mother Mary
comes to me (on a billboard in Puerto Rico)
holding a heart, bleeding like watercolors.
I look again, and she is a shaggy dog
smiling down from the pet food sign.

At an art show in Brown County, Indiana,
my eyes see only a blue Madonna
hand painted in a silver pendant.
I buy it to wear in the weeks before
my mother dies, and sometimes,
in my hour of darkness, she is standing
right in front of me hailing me like a cab.

I open my new used book of Bob Dylan
song lyrics, and find a prayer card
for Winifred McPherson's funeral
in Lincoln on December 23, 2004.
It marks "I Dreamed I Saw St. Augustine."
Holding the gentle heart of Jesus,
the Virgin peeks at me and winks.

Sixteen in Sixty Four

In the living room we are eating late,
fried chicken from the Elk's on metal trays
in front of the new black and white Philco
when we see Ed Sullivan introduce
the Beatles. I nearly choke on my fries
from excitement when they begin singing,
and when my dad leaves the room in disgust,
I weep confused tears. In my fantasy,
the lads shake their heads and look just at me.
In the hysteria of the era,
they want only to hold my willing hand.

On this night, all baby boomer sisters
bond from East to West, united by need,
by erotic energy. We become
a mob in knee socks, experiencing
a frenzy so visceral we'll feel it
fifty years later. We scream in desire,
memorize lyrics, write fan letters, play
45s: "Please Please Me" and "Love Me Do"
on little record players in our rooms.
We squirm in our bucket seats when we hear
"Yeah, yeah, yeaaah," come on the radio.

We seriously choose our favorite boy,
Paul nearly always because he is cute
beyond reason, but some switch for the sake
of sacred individuality
(although all of us wear penny loafers,
and skirts with dyed to match sweaters, all sleep
with rollers in our wet hair). But we each
need to be special. So some choose Ringo
just to be contrary, others warm up
to gentle George, and the beatniks in black
groove on John till finding out he's married.

It's fortuitous the Liverpool lads

don't take up Evil like Charles Manson
later will because we would be their gang
of millions slashing up America
for our Beatles. We adore them in that
scary "I'll do anything you want" way.
But they lead us in paths of righteousness,
offering spiritual awakening,
love, love, love and we will change as they do
twisting and shouting, giving peace a chance
throughout the rest of our fabulous lives.

Convalescence from Knee Surgery

I watch 65 episodes of Breaking Bad,
180 hours of the fall of Donald Trump,
deadhead 5000 petunias,
read 12 issues of the *New Yorker, Time, New York,*
three issues of *Vanity Fair, 92 Omaha World Heralds, 50 Norfolk Daily
Newses, 12 Missouri Valley Observers,* write 12 letters, 10 poems,
eat six watermelons, five bags of breadsticks, 66 green
smoothies (with spinach, blueberries, chia seeds,
ginger, carrots, avocado) 20 Colorado peaches, one BLT,
one catfish, eight salmon,15 root beer popsicles, 90 Diet Pepsis,
complete 200 crossword puzzles, 120 on-line jigsaw puzzles,
play 180 Scrabble games.

But who's counting?

Valentines

I create them with scissors and glue,
severing hearts from magazines,
painting drippy watercolored lips,
finding lockets and ribbons
for bare spots or edging,
and put them all on pages from old books,
yellowing and musty, thin and crinkly
like an old woman's skin, like her voice
calling out from a nursing home bed
to the lover whose heart stopped long ago.

I fashion empty boxes into keepsakes,
covering cardboard with comic strips
and Xeroxed photos arranged for a friend
who remembers the grade school thrill
of shoe boxes covered with crayoned names
and crepe paper hearts, a red and pink
receptacle for penny Valentines
from reluctant boys whose mothers make
them give one to every girl in the class
so no one is hurt, no one cries.

For the one I love, I rob an atlas
of maps of places with sweet memories for us,
collage them onto red paper, paste candy hearts
etched with messages:
MISS ME on India,
KISS ME on Blarney Castle, Ireland;
MARRY ME on Lincoln, Nebraska;
OOH LA LA on Paris where I fell in love
again and again like a choosy gold digger
ever stirred by new riches.

20/20

After cataract surgery my eyes
feel dry as the crackling leaves
in the garden, stuck to the wall.
Fall comes.

I see a face I don't know in the mirror,
blurry wrinkles now crisp, crow's feet:
Aunt Mattie's face, like cookie dough
crumbling under the rolling pin.

Myopia retouched my skin,
smoothing out the aging,
letting me believe in youth,
even with a senior discount.

Fall comes cruelly this year,
howling with tornadoes, wildfires,
scowling with its red temper tantrums,
golden and too rich like candy corn.
I see too well now, can't hide
in foggy vision from the blood
and guts of Halloween, of horror films,
from the fact that I am finite,
slowly crossing the icy path into winter,
trying to visualize how I will be—old.

Moonless 1973

I know late night after-parties,
black drives into the country
past cornstalks, unlatched
gates, chipping farmhouses
with wood stoves and dirty bathrooms.

No one notices newcomers,
music too loud, smoke too thick,
hosts too altered, Neil Young
too whiney, "a man needs a maid."
Beer abounds; some will share.

Some won't. Life's meaner
as this decade plunges ahead,
fewer peace signs, more flip offs.
Viet Nam vets coming home daily
pissed off and hurt.

Dreaded daybreak highlights dust
on the stereo, empty cigarette packs,
a dead mouse in the kitchen
where rancid butter sits
on a cracked linoleum counter.

October 29, 1962

Two days before Halloween
fifty years ago my parents
filled the washing machine
while my little brother
tried on his astronaut costume.
We would need water
if nuclear fallout was our treat,
if one of the bombs hit SAC
or the Minutemen missile silos buried
in South Dakota's prairie.

My father and mother went on a ride
in the '57 Chevy wagon
looking at Westside Park,
the Yankton College campus,
their old houses, places they
wanted to see one more time.
They visited their mothers,
prayed at their fathers' graves.

They came home and turned on tv,
black and white, and watched
in edgy silence as their president
and Khrushchev played a game
of end-of-our-world. They kissed
us goodnight, wondering if the Halloween
horror of burning flesh would be real
would be real in the morning . . .or not.

Storming on I-70

Lightning zig zags through thunder clouds
booming over me as torrential rain splashes
away visibility even as my windshield wipers
flap frantically, unable to keep up. I look
for exits, take 10 off 70, park with others
in a line of the fearful next to a brick Sinclair
station from the 40's. I believe I see tornadoes
dipping out of the black sky, and recall a family
story about Grandpa driving the family (with me
in my mother's arms) through South Dakota
to a birthday party during another June tempest.
Grandpa is praying the rosary, making the sign
of the cross in the old Nash sweet with the irises
for the festivities, deeply purple like bruised skies.

I imagine dying in a storm like this, struck by lightning
or another car, hydroplaning on a river road, blowing
away in a twister, sucked into clouds, contused
into the Land of Oz, cut by glass, broken by flying trees,
pelted by baseball-sized hail, rear ended by a semi,
drowned by hemorrhaging heavens. I can't entertain
such menacing day dreams, replaying in my mind
like CNN footage. After an hour, I drive on, seeing breaks
in the dark noon sky on my way home from Illinois
through Missouri where gas is fifty cents cheaper
and my flight may or may not be leaving from St. Louis.
I fill my tank, check my flight, all good, but now I suspect
humidity may kill me, and I do actually die for a few minutes
in the city before the shock of air conditioning
brings me back to life in Thrifty Rental Car's Shuttle.

Half Past Three (The Poet)

1911 oil on canvas

Chagall's subject looks at us upside down,
from red kaleidoscope eyes like Lucy-
in-the-sky's set in a kelly green head.
He contemplates writing a poem
and drinking a cuppa espresso
in the middle of this long night of wine,
absinthe possibly, (note his complexion).

He wears the sweet blue heart of an artist
outside his chest like an apron ready
to catch sprays of color or cubes of puke.
He understands the night, sees beauty
in shadowless rooms after lovers leave
with so much of the darkness still ahead.
Only a cat lapping his arm shows us
he is loved.

Chicago Blues

I sit in front of Chagall's stained glass
American Windows sketching one
indigo panel after another:
random hands, yellow moons, purple bird,
lit menorah, ballet feet, magenta masks
all startling the blue here and there,
overwhelming me with details of beauty.

Warhol's Mao looms large on one wall
in Contemporary Art. The original
photo shows an enemy of individualism,
but Andy has popped pink rouge
on his cheeks, stroked lime green
on his titular jacket, and shaded his eyes
in shadow the color of a lapis necklace.

I stare at Picasso's Old Guitarist
as a guide tells students to look closely
for the woman above his left ear,
a ghost painted on the canvas first,
forsaken for this masterpiece.
I don't find her, lost as we both are
in the angles, the compassion, the blues.

Summer of Love

Not yet twenty,

I fell in love with everything
mid-nineteen sixty-seven:
radical new style, long summer-
blonde hair, flower tiaras,
music loud and anti-war,
wrap-around minis in soft suede,
scrappy sandals, turquoise moccasins
from the rez, Mexican huaraches,
fringed leather purses hanging
from skinny sunburned arms,
pale pink lipstick, fringy headbands,
crocheted wedding gowns,
(ivory with no slips),
haltered shower dresses
(hot pink or paisley without a bra)
showing off brown shoulders, wild prints of pink
and teal, purple and tangerine,
never too much.

Missing Winnie

Invitations to the birthday party
arrive in the mail of every fourth grade
girl in Lincoln School except the Native girl
who isn't invited because of that.

Cousins come, too, and we hide behind masks
and pin the tail on a paper donkey,
eat cake baked in the immigrant grandma's
kitchen, whipped cream smearing faces.

Gifts are given, received, ripped open,
oohed and aahed over, and thanked for
in picture Christmas cards of little girls
lined up by height: Polly Ann Jean Jan
Carol Caren Elizabeth Lila Linda—
like ten little Indians minus the real one.

Karen Breaks an Arm at a Gas Station in Uruguay

I.
just the facts, maam

Because I want a Diet Pepsi, I squirm out
from the backseat of the two-door Chevy.
My foot catches on a seat cover, and I sprawl
left arm first *wowoo* forehead *wawa* right arm *owow*
onto the concrete parking lot of a Petrobras
service station. I'm hurt, I say, and some guys roll me over.
I feel wind on my belly and want to pull my inadequate shirt
over my gall bladder scar which sits like an albino anchovy
above my waist. I lie still, Wes over me,
teeth chattering, while men chat, call an ambulance
and the U.S. Consulate. One of the men talks
about the Nebraska Medical Center,
his parents living in Potter as I whimper and nod.
The EMT's are women.
I am tied down.
I am thirsty.
I am exposed.
I am hauled.

II.
tripping

My head sparkles, my kaleidoscope
eyes follow bright lights, see the Southern Cross
for the first time near a crescent moon
smiling crookedly high above Montevideo;
and I'm wheeled into the ER for x-rays
at the British Hospital where my doctor
kisses his nurse before removing my earrings
and necklace, one, two, three, four rings
he counts, dropping them into a little plastic bag,
twinkling in my swelling right hand;
and handsome Latinos hug me, say *amor*,
give me chocolate because it heals;

and I hear the tango, which takes two,
Wes and Karen, into its good arms;
and Sister Morphine runs through my veins
like a rock and roll princess jogging

on the white sand of Rio de la Plata
on whose waves I float off
into Fall in May,
a world upside down.

50th Reunion

"The Frontal-Temporal Dementia affects planning, organizing, expressive and receptive language, under-standing of numbers, etc. The Alzheimer's variant affects short term memory. She also has Posterior Cortical Atrophy which is increasingly affecting her ability to process what she sees."

She fights four demons, dementia tripled,
and brittle diabetes, but still wants to see
her high school class. She was valedictorian,
college graduate in three years, *summa cum laude.*

She fixes her hair, asks for setting gel.
that's right in front of her.
I say, "There, the silver bottle,"
and she picks up the hairdryer.

She doesn't want to go to the football game
so we go to the meet and greet at the Landing.
She sees her best friend Claudia
and both cry. My tears are waiting.

She wants to see everyone, grows tired
of having no words. Looks at me
for what to do. We leave early. She worries
about the insulin she can no longer shoot.

At the banquet everyone talks to her.
She smiles the whole night. We take
lots of pictures; she tries to hold thoughts
long enough to tell a story.

And when she says goodbye
to old friends who will probably
attend 55th or 60th reunions, and so on,
I know that she will not.

Christmas Cookies

I eat the burned ones, inevitable
like the chirping in a smoke detector
when its battery dies. Every year
I stir up my Butter Is Better recipe
that won 2nd place at the 2nd level
 in the eighth grade science fair.

I bake seven dozen at 400 degrees,
crisp sugar cookies with a touch
of lemon rind and red and green sugar
sprinkled on top. The third sheet usually burns.
along with my hand, but this time
just the cookies.

I will not throw them away, knowing how
little of my life I want to devote to baking.
That time is up for this yuletide. So I eat
them even though friends say carbon
will give me cancer, even though charred
sweetness stays on my tongue for a long time.

I think it began as penance, sinful
waste of sugar and butter; but now
I'm almost happy having my own little batch
(this year eight) to crunch.

November After We Stop Saving Daylight

"Turn, turn, turn" the Byrds

I'm driving home from Illinois on the day
after we turned our clocks back an hour.
The sky's the color of tarnishing sterling
and drizzle dampens my view of highway signs.
I'm trying to get to Peoria before nightfall,
and this afternoon that means too soon.
Driving 80 on 74, I regret the hours I've lost
with my family and the hours I will gain
in the Hampton Inn by the Pair-a-Dice Casino.
I take a wrong turn away from the river.

Last night I turned the clock forward instead of back
even though I knew better, and my granddaughters
went to sleep at seven-thirty.
Rudy, their dog, is dying. He lay on a brown blanket
in the dark garage, and I gave him a pill
wrapped up in American cheese; we looked
sadly into each other's eyes. I sat down beside him
and told him he'd been a good dog, that I may not
see him again. I told him he had been gentle
with the little girls and that he always protected us.

I dim the lights and pull up the hotel's white duvet,
chilled to the bone, gray static cackling from the TV
I can't work. I play Free Cell solitaire on my computer
and wonder if the housekeeper changed the alarm clock
beside my bed. Tomorrow I will get up at six in the dark
(which would have been five a couple days ago)
and take off at sunrise whenever that will be.
I will cross several dusky rivers and reach home
by three o'clock in the afternoon which would have
been four if we hadn't given away our light.

Four Ways of Looking at Flakes

I.
Ice from snow from rain settles on the sidewalk
like a pixie rink in a fairy tale,
making the trek to the morning paper tricky.
My feet snug in slippers slip,
flakes fall into nose and eyelashes,
fill the pockets of my robe.

An orange bag secured with a rubber band
protects the World Herald from the blizzard,
which has buried it in a drift.
News of the day can't be so important,
but I skate along for the puzzles
in my daily quest to find solutions.

II.
Pink fiberglass holds my broken bone in place.
Underneath, red surgery stitches, pale arm,
ashy skin in need of a loofah wait.
Inside, the bones don't care,
tending to themselves,
healing at a pace none can predict.

They leave the flesh
to layer like puff pastry,
dead over dead cells
building up to a snow storm
of purification when they slough off
after a dismal drill splits the cast.

III.
The lavender and yellow wallpaper in my bedroom
peels as I lie there at night in my flannel pajamas
thinking about first grade.
Although I am told not to, I can't resist
stripping bits from the wall,
watching the transformation.

Flakes of paste and paper fall under the bed
like dead moths as I keep trying to find
what is underneath,
what rot is covered up,
what nightmares exist
in this house my mother hates.

IV.
My best friends and I argue about whether
to put sugar on milked or dry cereal.
We love Raisin Bran and Shredded Wheat,
spoonfuls of sweet, wet flakes.
I like to taste the granules, not mix them up;
she likes stirring sugar into milk.

We are only seven and don't have much
to disagree about, only the best color for eyes,
if paying cash (her) or charging (me) is better,
whether to wear underwear to bed,
if margarine or butter is better,
and if Captain Kangaroo equals Howdy Doody.

Airborne

In the early morning hours of the day
my father dies, he sits on the floor
disorganizing war papers and sports
memorabilia, photographs he shot
in a plane over occupied Paris
that pour out of a drawer in his nightstand.

He leans on his cane, left arm strong,
but which will break in several hours
when he tries to get out of bed alone,
falling instead, during a final stab
at independence in his new narrow
world of total nursing care.

By the bed where his second daughter
 will hear his last breath,
he sleeps fractured.
She drives recklessly from Illinois
to St. Louis, flies on Delta an hour
to Eppley, speeds to Yankton where he waits.

At the feeder he filled with sunflower seeds
outside his window, finches flap, sensing
a soul's indecision. He holds his wings
inside until he sees her again,
until she steps in, opens the window
and clears him to fly.

Blue

Turquoise moccasins wrapped in Santa paper
wait under a tree in Tucson where my sister
lies in a hospital bed unaware.
The size sevens were bought at Al's Oasis,
outpost on the way to the Black Hills,
her favorite place, though she may not remember.

They remind me of a log house in Custer
State Park. We were ten and eight and our mother
had bought us jeans lined in red plaid flannel
from Duhamel's Western Store. We stayed
in the pine-forested cabin of friends
whose boys locked us in the outhouse.

If she could be herself, we would comment
on these memories, get out the pictures
of me with a perm squinting into the sun
by our father who looks like James Dean,
of her standing by the Chevy wagon happy,
her mind clear and full of promise.

In Convenient Care

Many sad sacks sit in the waiting room
dark bags under eyes, Kleenex-stuffed pockets.
TV blares horror sniffy kids shouldn't see
Everyone doesn't know something: birthdate,
insurance number, name of a new drug.

I sit in a corner trying not to breathe
anyone else's air, touch anything.
I place my purse between me and the frowner
beside me waiting to hear my name called,
afraid I won't with stuffy ears.

The seven-year-old in a green t-shirt
with a cat Statue of Liberty sits with her grandma,
a woman with a raccoon tail slipped into her belt,
who tells the nurse she has no money and leaves.
Guy in Huskers shirt doesn't have the copay.

We are the Sinus Infection Club
 who may have died a century ago
or just gone to bed miserable,
no aspirin, antibiotics, Afrin,
no neti-pots, or Tylenol P.M.

Karen Wingett grew up on the rolling prairie of South Dakota near the Missouri River. She earned a B.A. in English from Yankton College and an M.A. in English from the University of South Dakota and taught many years beginning in St. Mary's School for Indian Girls and later in Norfolk, Nebraska until her retirement. She joined a writing group and continued her love affair with poetry which began when she was a teenager.

Wingett received an Individual Artist Fellowship from the Nebraska Arts Council. Her work has appeared in *Mid-America Poetry Review*, the anthologies *Times of Sorrow, Times of Grace* and *An Untidy Season* (Backwaters Press). Her chapbook, *Tap Dancing at the Corn Palace,* was published by Finishing Line Press.

She and her husband Wes collect books and antiques, watch community college basketball games and travel all over the world. Her son, daughter-in-law, and three granddaughters delight and inspire her.